JAMAICA

A TRUE BOOK®

by
Ann Heinrichs

Children's Press®
A Division of Scholastic Inc.

New York Toronto London Auckland Sydney
Mexico City New Delhi Hong Kong
Danbury, Connecticut

A Jamaican girl
drinks "cold jelly"—
a chilled coconut.

Content Consultant
Professor Kit Belgum
*Department of
Germanic Studies
University of Texas
at Austin*

Reading Consultant
Nanci R. Vargus, Ed.D.
*Assistant Professor
Literacy Education
University of Indianapolis
Indianapolis, IN*

*The photograph on the title
pages shows
a market scene.*

Library of Congress Cataloging-in-Publication Data

Heinrichs, Ann
    Jamaica / by Ann Heinrichs.
        p. cm. — (A True book)
Summary: An introduction to the geography, history, economy, people,
and social life and customs of Jamaica, an island nation in the Caribbean
Sea.
Includes bibliographical references and index.
    ISBN 0-516-22676-2 (lib. bdg.)   0-516-27751-0 (pbk.)
    1. Jamaica—Juvenile literature. [1. Jamaica.] I. Title. II. Series.
F1868.2.H45 2003
972.92—dc21

                                                            2001008506

Contents

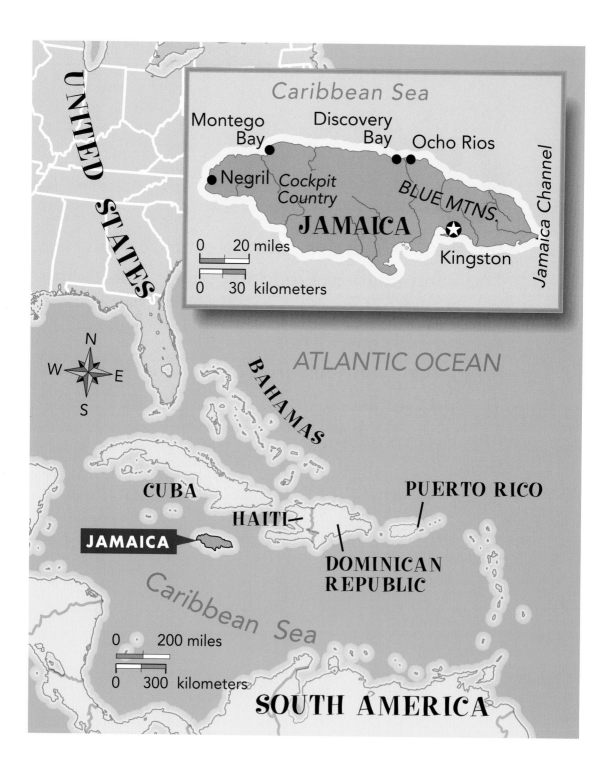

Beaches, Mountains, and Forests

Jamaica is a beautiful island nation in the Caribbean Sea. It lies about halfway between Florida and South America. Jamaica's nearest neighbors are Cuba and Haiti.

Jamaica is a land of sparkling beaches, misty mountains, and

Beach resorts attract many tourists to Jamaica.

deep forests. Miles of white, sandy beaches line its coast. Other coastal areas are covered with forests, grasslands, and swamps.

From the coast, the land gradually rises up to a plateau, or high, level ground. The western plateau is called Cockpit Country. It is marked by underground caves and deep holes called cockpits.

High mountains rise in the center of the island. They are covered with thick forests. Waterfalls splash down the mountainside into rushing streams. The Blue Mountains in the east are Jamaica's highest peaks. The mountaintops are often hidden in blue-gray clouds.

The Blue Lagoon
near Port Antonio

The forests along the coast
are thick with bamboo and
thorny bushes. Tall mahogany
and ebony trees rise high
above them. Climbing vines
wind around tree trunks, and

orchids hang from branches. Cactuses grow in the dry southwest. In the swamps, crocodiles slink among the mangrove trees.

The mountain forests are full of wildlife. Wild pigs, mongooses, lizards, and bats find shelter there. A little

Thousands of bats live in Jamaica's forests and caves.

animal called the *hutia* scurries across the rocky hills. It is partly like a rat and partly like a guinea pig. Hutias have lived in Jamaica for hundreds of years. Streamertail hummingbirds dart through the trees. Their

A streamertail hummingbird, Jamaica's national bird

two long, black tail feathers sweep behind them. Giant swallowtail butterflies flit through the forest too. They are the largest butterflies in the Western Hemisphere.

Jamaica's climate is warm all year long. There are two rainy seasons. One occurs in May and June. The other occurs around September and October. Hurricanes sometimes sweep in from the ocean.

Jamaica's government is working to protect its natural

areas. Forests once covered almost the whole island. Now, however, less than half of the forestlands remain. European settlers cut down thousands of trees to clear the land for farming. In modern times, pollution has also become a problem. Many coastal areas are polluted with waste from factories and from humans. Both pollution and the loss of forests are dangerous for Jamaica's wildlife.

The Long Road to Freedom

Arawak Indians have lived in Jamaica for hundreds of years. They called their home *Xaymaca*, meaning "land of wood and water." In time, this word became Jamaica. The Arawak lived in large villages under a *cacique*, or chief. They fished the coastal waters and grew corn and *cassava*, a plant used in cooking.

Christopher Columbus was the first European to reach Jamaica. Sailing from Spain, he landed in Jamaica in 1494. Soon other Spaniards arrived. They put the Arawak to work as slaves on their farms and ranches and in the mines. However, the Arawak eventually died out. They were victims of overwork and European diseases.

Next, the Spaniards began bringing African slaves to work

the land. Slavery would be a major part of Jamaican life for more than three hundred years. Some of the slaves escaped into the mountains. They were called Maroons. The name comes from the Spanish word *cimarrón*, meaning "wild" or "untamed."

A Maroon Festival held outside of Montego Bay

The British captured Jamaica in 1655 and began driving out the Spaniards. The British also made Jamaica a safe refuge for pirates. The pirates helped the British by attacking Spanish ships and towns. By 1670, the British had full control of the island. They raised sugarcane on large farms called plantations. They also grew coffee, cotton, and indigo—a plant used to make a blue dye.

At this time, sugar was becoming very popular in England, France, and other European countries. Raising sugarcane was

Sugarcane has been an important crop since the 1600s.

very profitable for Jamaica and many neighboring islands.

Under British rule, Jamaica became one of the busiest slave-trading centers in the world. British ships brought hundreds of thousands of slaves from Africa. Some slaves were put to work in Jamaica, while others were sold to people in other plantation regions. By the 1700s, most of the people in Jamaica were slaves.

The slaves were poorly fed and clothed. Men, women, and children often labored twelve hours a day in the fields. Punishments were harsh. A slave could be beaten, whipped, or killed for even a small offense. Over the years, many slave **rebellions** broke out.

Jamaica's slaves were officially freed in 1838. Thousands of workers were brought to Jamaica from India and China to work the plantations and build railroads for low wages. Meanwhile, most of the former slaves lived in poverty. Some started small farms of their own. Many kept working on plantations for low wages. They were still overworked and abused, and not much better off than they had been as slaves. People of mixed European and African ancestry had a better life. Some ran farms, while others started successful businesses. They soon formed a thriving middle class.

At this time, Jamaica had a House of Assembly that governed the island. However, only landowners and wealthy business-men could vote and hold office.

In 1865, black and mixed-race Jamaicans staged the Morant Bay Rebellion. They wanted fair treat-ment and voting rights for all. The government executed hundreds of people who took part in the rebellion. Then, in 1866, Great Britain made Jamaica a crown **colony**. Under this system, Britain appointed Jamaica's governor and lawmakers.

In 1944, after years of struggle, all adult Jamaicans got the right to vote. This included people of all races and classes, rich and poor alike. Jamaica gained full independence from Great Britain in 1962.

Princess Margaret makes a speech at the ceremony granting independence to the former British colony of Jamaica.

Today, Jamaica's prime minister is the head of government. A governor-general represents the British king or queen. However, he or she does not have real governing power. Jamaica's Parliament is its lawmaking body. It consists of a House of Representatives and a Senate. Voters elect their representatives, while the governor-general appoints the senators. Jamaica is also a member of

Jamaica's prime minister,
P.J. Patterson

the Commonwealth of
Nations. This is a union of
former British colonies.

National Heroes

Jamaica honors seven people as national heroes:

Nanny of the Maroons (?–1833) was a fierce warrior. She led the Maroons in fighting the British in the 1700s.

Samuel Sharpe (1801–1832) led a large slave rebellion in 1831. This helped bring about the end of slavery in Jamaica.

Paul Bogle (1822?– 1865) was a Baptist preacher. He was executed for leading the Morant Bay Rebellion in 1865.

George William Gordon (1820–1865) was a free black landowner who served in Jamaica's House of Assembly. He urged Jamaicans to protest against the unjust conditions under which they lived.

Marcus Garvey (1887–1940), called the Black Moses, led an African nationalist movement. He taught blacks to be proud of their African heritage. Rastafarians adopted many of his teachings.

Norman Manley (1893–1969) worked to help poor laborers. He helped get voting rights for Jamaicans in 1944.

Alexander Bustamante (1884–1977) worked for Jamaican independence. He became Jamaica's first prime minister in 1962.

People gather around Norman Manley, founder of the Jamaican People's National Party, as he makes his way to the cathedral for Jamaica's Independence Day celebrations.

The People of Jamaica

Jamaica is home to more than two-and-a-half million people. About half of them live in cities and towns. The largest cities lie on the coast. Kingston, the nation's capital, is Jamaica's biggest city. Other large cities are Spanish Town and Montego Bay.

Many different people from diverse **cultures** settled in Jamaica throughout its history. They include East Indian, Chinese, Syrian, English, German, and Portuguese people. Today, more than nine out of ten Jamaicans are descended from African slaves. Most are purely African, while others are people of mixed ancestry.

English is Jamaica's official language. However, most

Jamaicans speak Jamaican Creole, or **patois**. This is a version of English with African, Spanish, and French words and sounds mixed in.

The **majority** of Jamaicans are Christians. Jewish people have a long history in Jamaica too. They began settling on the island in the 1600s. Jamaica also has small Hindu and Muslim communities.

Some Jamaicans follow native beliefs. They include

Worshipers enter a Jamaican church.

These Jamaicans belong to the Rastafarian sect.

sects that combine Christianity and African traditions. Another local religious movement is Rastafarianism. It gained many followers in the 1950s.

Rastafarianism

Rastafarianism is a religious sect named for Haile Selassie. He was the emperor of Ethiopia in Africa from 1930 to 1974. Before becoming emperor, his name was Ras Tafari. Early Rastafarians saw Haile Selassie as a god. Rastafarianism draws

Haile Selassie was seen by many poor Jamaicans as the savior of all of the world's African descendants.

many of its beliefs from the teachings of Marcus Garvey. He urged blacks to be self-reliant and proud of their African heritage. Many Rastafarians wear loose-fitting robes and wear their hair in ropelike strands called **dreadlocks.**

Black leader Marcus Garvey, president of the Negro Improvement Association whose teaching influenced Rastafarianism.

A Land of Many Riches

Tourists love Jamaica's sunny climate and sparkling beaches. They enjoy hiking through the lush mountains and forests. Kingston, Ocho Rios, Negril, and Montego Bay are the most popular spots to visit. Tourism is very important to the Jamaican economy. It brings a lot of money into the country.

Dunn's River Falls is a popular tourist spot near Ocho Rios.

Cutting sugarcane (above) and Blue Mountain coffee beans (right)

Farming is still a major business in Jamaica. Sugarcane and bananas are the most important crops. The sugarcane is made into sugar, molasses, and rum. Jamaicans also grow citrus fruits, yams, coffee, cacao, tobacco, and spices. Jamaica's Blue Mountain coffee is considered one of the best coffees in the world. Cacao beans are made into chocolate and cocoa butter.

Bauxite mining is a big part of Jamaican industry.

Jamaica is one of the world's leading producers of bauxite, which is made into aluminum. Jamaica's sandy beaches are a mineral source too. The sand contains silica, which is made into glass. Jamaica's gypsum is made into construction materials.

Factories in Jamaica make good use of local products. They use Jamaican farm products and minerals to make sugar, cloth, chemicals, metals, cement, and many other goods.

A cement factory in Kingston

Food, Fun, and Folklore

Jamaicans eat many delicious foods that grow on the island. Yams, breadfruits, mangoes, pineapples, bananas, and plantains are all home grown. Rice with red beans is a popular Jamaican dish. So is jerk meat, which is spicy grilled chicken or pork.

Many Jamaican foods came from other cultures. A bright-red

Collecting bananas (top left), the akee plant (bottom left), and a Jamaican street vendor serving grilled meat (below)

fruit called *akee* came from West Africa. Akee and saltfish is a favorite breakfast dish. People from India brought spicy dishes flavored with curry. *Bammy* is a cassava bread that was made by the Arawak Indians. The British introduced fruitcake.

Reggae is Jamaica's most famous music. Bob Marley helped to make reggae popular all over the world.

Cricket is Jamaica's national sport. It is played with a ball and a flat, paddlelike bat. The British introduced this game during colonial days.

Soccer is almost as popular as cricket. Jamaicans are proud of the Reggae Boyz, their national soccer team. In 1998,

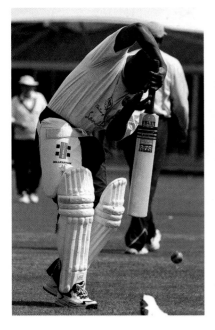

A cricket player (left) and a marching band on Independence Day (above)

they played in the World Cup soccer finals.

Jamaicans celebrate their Independence Day on the first Monday in August. Song and dance events and contests lead up to the day. The festival ends with a costume show and grand parade.

Jonkonnu dancing is a Christmas **tradition**. It began among Jamaica's African slaves. Dancers wear colorful costumes and spectacular masks. They sing and dance to the rhythm of drums, banjos, and other instruments.

Jamaican folklore is rich with African traditions. *Anansi*, from West African folklore, is a spider man who can take many forms. He plays tricks on people to teach them lessons. *Obeah* is a force that can do good or evil. To avoid

One Jamaican tradition is a three to four day celebration called Cudjoe Day. Also known as Treaty Day, it is celebrated by Maroons on January 6 of each year.

obeah, a Jamaican tries not to be too proud about good health or good fortune.

Jamaicans are proud of who they are. Their culture and traditions bring joy and meaning to everyday life.

To Find Out More

Here are some additional resources to help you learn more about Jamaica:

 **Books**

Allen, Beryl M. **Jamaica: A Junior History.** Heinemann, 1993.

Barraclough, John. **Jamaica.** Rigby Interactive Library, 1996.

Brownlie, Allison. **Jamaica.** Raintree/Steck Vaughn, 1998.

Dolan, Sean. **Bob Marley.** Chelsea House, 1997.

Hausman, Gerald. **Duppy Talk: West Indian Tales of Mystery and Magic.** Simon and Schuster, 1994.

Rojany, Lisa (editor). **The Magic Feather: A Jamaican Legend.** Troll Associates, 1995.

Sheehan, Sean. **Jamaica.** Marshall Cavendish, 1994.

Wilkins, Frances. **Jamaica.** Chelsea House, 1999.

Organizations and Online Sites

Jamaica Tourist Board
500 N. Michigan Ave.
Suite 1030
Chicago, IL 60611
312-527-1296

Discover Jamaica!
*http://www.discover
jamaica.com*

For information on
Jamaica's cities, customs,
history, government, and
economy.

Introduction to Jamaica
*http://luna.cas.usf.edu/
~alaing/jamaica.html*

To learn about Jamaica's
culture, traditions, and
folklore.

Embassy of Jamaica
http://www.emjamusa.org

For information about
Jamaica's government,
economy, people, culture,
and much more.

Important Words

colony a territory that belongs to the country that controls it

culture the beliefs, customs, and way of life of a group of people

dreadlocks hairstyle consisting of matted or braided ropelike sections

majority the greater part of a whole

patois a form of speech that combines different languages

rebellion an uprising to protest unacceptable conditions

reggae popular Jamaican music that combines rock and native sounds

sect a religious or political group with distinctive beliefs

tradition a custom common among a family or group

Index

Meet the Author

Ann Heinrichs grew up in Arkansas and currently lives in Chicago, Illinois. She has written more than eighty books about American, European, Asian, and African history and culture. Several of her books have won national and regional awards.

Besides the United States, she has traveled in Europe, North Africa, the Middle East, and East Asia. The desert is her favorite terrain.

Ms. Heinrichs holds a B.A. and an M.A. in piano performance. She practices t'ai chi empty-hand and sword forms and has won many awards in martial arts competitions.

Photographs © 2003: A Perfect Exposure/Randa Bishop: 1; Corbis Images: 43 (Tony Arruza), 10 (Hans Dieter Brandl/Frank Lane Picture Agnecy), 17 (Manuela Höfer), 31 top (Hulton-Deutsch Collection), 39 right (Layne Kennedy), 41 right (Danny Lehman), 29; Getty Images/Ray Stubblebine/Reuters: 23; HultonlArchive/Getty Images: 21, 25; ImageState/Michael Ventura: 6; Masterfile/Greg Stott: 8; North Wind Picture Archives: 39 top left; Peter Arnold Inc./Russell C. Hansen: 9; PhotoEdit/Richard Lord: 34 top; Photri Inc.: 39 bottom left (Ellsworth), 33 (Dennis MacDonald); Stock Boston/Willie L. Hill Jr.: 37; The Image Works: 15 (Hinata Haga/HAGA), 30, 31 bottom, 41 left (Topham); W. Lynn Seldon Jr.: 34 bottom; Woodfin Camp & Associates: cover (Susan Lapides), 2 (Paula Lerner), 36 (Leroy Woodson).

Map by Joe LeMonnier